Welcome to the wonderful world of mother daughter book clubs!

The enclosed 80-page booklet is excerpted from *The Mother Daughter Book Club*, a book I wrote with and for my daughters. We hope that you will be inspired by our story to start your own mother daughter book club, a rewarding new twist on an age-old form of entertainment. The section called *Why Start a Mother Daughter Book Club* discusses how books can bring people together in a meaningful, fun way, whether as a group activity or simply one mother and her daughter reading and talking about a book.

Then we provide you with the basics of how to organize your own book club. While aimed mostly at 9- to 14-year-olds, the ideas and suggestions work through senior year of high school. Although originally written for mothers and girls, the material presented is easily adaptable to any adult-child combination: Father-son, grandparent-grandchild, and mentor-mentee book clubs are all now part of the movement started by our book, first published 10 years ago and now revised and expanded.

You will find a sampling from the full-length book of reading lists, profiles of club members, and practical tips covering all aspects of keeping a club running smoothly. Perhaps most helpful is the sample discussion guide, which is intended to help you create your own discussion guides for the carefully chosen books in this set. Club members not only make up discussion questions, we dream up activities that relate to the book, like games and crafts and, of course, good snacks. As you will discover, it is not as difficult as you might have thought; in fact, we always let the girl who is hosting the meeting come up with the questions and lead the meeting's discussion.

So, turn off the television and computers, just for a while, and ask your daughter to have a chat. Together decide which interesting, enjoyable book will be your first book club pick. Choose a date, make a list of possible members, and send out your invites.

Let the reading—and bonding—begin!

Shireen Dodson
Morgan Fykes (21)
Skylar Fykes (16)

Praise for

THE MOTHER-DAUGHTER BOOK CLUB

"What a great idea! . . . I hope the idea will spread."
—*Beverly Cleary*

"A wonderful idea."
—*Ann M. Martin, author of the Baby-sitter's Club series*

"This is a book that was waiting to be born, an angel book sent to give mothers and daughters hope. *The Mother-Daughter Book Club* is about community, about adults supporting each other and helping other people's children."
—*Mary Pipher, Ph.D., author of* Reviving Ophelia

"*The Mother-Daughter Book Club* is an idea that is so wonderful, so full of commonsense goodness, why has it taken so long for it to be born? This could easily be the catalyst for a national movement."
—*Jim Trelease, author of* The Read-Aloud Handbook

The

MOTHER-DAUGHTER
Book Club Kit

First Harper paperback published 2007.

Designed by Nancy Singer Olaguera/ISPN Publishing Services

Library of Congress Cataloging-in-Publication Data has been applied for.

ISBN: 978-0-06-144934-5 (pbk.)
ISBN-10: 0-06-144934-2 (pbk.)

07 08 09 10 11   ISPN/RRD   10 9 8 7 6 5 4 3 2 1

To my daughter and my friend Morgan,
who was the inspiration for it all;
to my daughter Skylar,
for continuing the journey;
and to my son, Leroy III,
who reminds me that it is all a blessing

PREFACE

Ten years ago, in the fall of 1996, I started a mother-daughter book club with my daughter Morgan. The following February, in celebration of Black History Month, a reporter who knew one of the moms wrote a wonderful human interest story about our Mother-Daughter Book Club. The story mentioned that I worked at the Smithsonian Institution, and my phone at work began to ring off the hook. People wanted to join my Mother-Daughter Club; they wanted to talk about what a great idea they thought a mother-daughter book club was, and if they could not join my club, they wanted to know how to start their own mother-daughter book club. The response was so overwhelming that I started collecting contact information with a promise to send a one-page write-up on how to start a mother-daughter book club. So when eventually I received a phone call from an agent asking, "Have you ever thought about writing a book?" I was prepared. In 1997 *The Mother-Daughter Book Club* was published.

Many pages later, Morgan's younger sister, Skylar, watched and waited to have her own Mother-Daughter Book Club. She and I began the Bookworms when the girls were eight and in the third grade, just starting to read chapter books. Thinking that girls so young could not sustain a meaningful discussion, we added a related craft activity to the meetings. Were we ever wrong! The discussions, though shorter, were rich and insightful. The Bookworms stayed together for six years, into the beginning of eighth grade. As they anxiously anticipated high school, their activities became more centered on their individual schools and the Bookworms drifted apart. I mourned the loss of my secret weapon for getting through the difficult high school years. Had we laid enough foundation? Who was I going to discuss books with?

I received my answer to those questions in the fall of 2004, when Skylar entered high school and I found myself at the back-to-school potluck for ninth graders. A mom new to the area mentioned that she had read my book several years before. She regretted that as her girls' childhoods were waning, she had never followed through on her intention to participate in a mother-daughter book club. She wondered if it was too late for the girls to be interested in such a club. That was all it took for me to galvanize and start an all-new group with and for our daughters who were all just entering high school. Once again Skylar pulled together a wonderful group of ten girls who shared an enthusiasm and passion for reading. The girls all attend Georgetown Day School, known for its academic rigor; but somehow they always manage to juggle their book club reading, schoolwork, and extracurricular activities. They come each month ready to tackle tough issues and their insights never cease to cause the moms to pass secret silent smiles of relief from one to another. Our girls are growing up just fine!

Meanwhile, in the summer of 2005, I received another phone call, this time from my publisher, saying, "You know, it's been almost ten years—have you thought about updating *The Mother-Daughter Book Club*?" It seemed impossible that ten years had flown by. So much in my own life had changed: My son had graduated from college and answered the call into ministry; Morgan, who was my original catalyst, was twenty and a college sophomore; my role with my aging parents had reversed, as I was now caring for them; I was separated from my husband of twenty-seven years; and Skylar was no longer the baby but a nearly grown young lady. The one constant through it all was the joy that I experienced from reading and sharing books with my daughters.

When I received the call to do a new edition, I had just finished year one of Skylar's new Mother-Daughter Club. I was fully immersed again in the world of young adult literature, talking, laughing, and learning through books. It felt wonderful. So it was without hesitation that I agreed to this tenth anniversary edition of *The Mother-Daughter Book Club* in which you will get to know Skylar and the other members of Skylar's Mother-Daughter Book Club. The voices of the very first Mother-Daughter Book Club, which lasted until the older girls went off to college, are still here of course. At our annual Christmas holiday reunion the original members looked back on their book club years, and their reflections have been added as well. But you will also meet the members of Skylar's club, who give new meaning to just how special a Mother-Daughter Book Club can be.

The world has changed a lot in the past ten years. Oprah started her famous television book club, and adult book clubs became hugely popular. J. K. Rowling introduced Harry Potter and children's literature has not been the same. Girls—and to everyone's amazement, boys—were suddenly racing through 700-page books with complete rapture. This new edition includes complete discussion guides for books we've discovered in recent years—books that deal with terrorism and peer pressure and all manner of topics of interest to a more grown-up generation of mother-daughter readers. And this book has inspired thousands of mother-daughter book clubs around the world! Not a week goes by that I do not hear from some mom who has discovered the joys and is reaping the benefits of participating in a mother-daughter book club. Some of their heartwarming stories are included in this tenth anniversary edition. It is wonderful to have a place where girls can be girls, and explore their present lives while dreaming out loud about their futures.

With this book, I invite you to join us in Mother-Daughter Book Club country. I think you will agree that a one-page write-up would never have been adequate to capture the beauty and magic of this very special place.

Shireen Dodson
2007

ONE

Why Start a Mother-Daughter Book Club?

TO OUR MOTHERS AND GRANDMOTHERS, AUNTS AND GREAT-AUNTS. TO ALL THE WOMEN WHO STOOD BEFORE US, TELLING US ABOUT WHERE THEY CAME FROM, WHAT THEY SAID, DID, AND IMAGINED. THEY LET US KNOW THEY STOOD FOR US. TALKING, THEY COMBED OUR HAIR, ROCKED US TO SLEEP, SANG TO US, TOLD US TALES OF THEN AND NOW—AND TOMORROW. THEY WORRIED ABOUT US. THEY HOPED FOR US AND SHOWED US THE WAY. THEY CARED.

—VIRGINIA HAMILTON, *dedication*, Her Stories

Morgan Fykes & The Original Mother-Daughter Book Club

Hello. My name is Morgan Fykes. When I started the book club with my mother, Shireen Dodson, I was nine years old. Two years later we were publishing a book and doing a book tour together. Since then a lot has changed between my mother and me. The older I get, the more our relationship has become a friendship. We've been through a lot together in these past ten years: deaths in the family, seeing my friends' parents and now my own parents separate, and of course high school, which was a unique experience. While change can be hard, we have gotten through it all with grace, and I cannot imagine how different our relationship would be had we never had the book club. It is not just the relationship that I have developed with my mom that has changed my life growing up; it is also the closeness I have with my friends' moms. I would never hesitate to pick up the phone and call them if I ever needed anything. That is an amazing feeling. Another wonderful aspect of the book club was that it included people from different aspects of my life so I have been able to maintain relationships with people that I might otherwise have lost touch with over the years.

Over the life of our club, mother-daughter pairs moved away and others lost interest and dropped out. We wanted to make sure we would always have a critical mass when we met so over the years we added new members: Jennifer Green and her mom, Cheryl; Shannon Sanders and her mom, Monice; Brittany Lattisaw and her mom, Ardawn; Nikki Jourdain-Earl and her mom, Judy; Rachel Charity and her mom, Gail; and Mariel Fernandez and her mom, Nurial, all joined us on our journey.

I am now twenty years old and a sophomore at Cornell College in Iowa where my majors are Psychology and possibly Business. I am currently treasurer of the Black Awareness Culture Organization at my school as well as a member of the cheerleading squad and the women's golf team. I work on the Alumni Phone-a-thon, which is a blast because

I get to talk to students from the past about Cornell. The most interesting are the people who attended Cornell before the OCAAT (One Course at a Time) was instituted. OCAAT is what attracted me to Cornell. You take one class at a time for three and a half weeks and then you have fours days off (Block Break). After each block break, you start all over again with a new class. Since most of the classes are capped at twenty-five students, I enjoy a classroom setting that is personal and intimate. Cornell is a great fit for me because it works really well for how I learn.

While our book club is no longer active, we have started having an annual holiday party during our Christmas break from college. It is a fun time, where we all get together and talk about what everyone has been doing and current issues in our lives. This year we even pulled out some of the old tapes from the first book tour. It was a great time for all the girls and moms to relax and catch up.

Here is what some of the voices throughout the book are now doing: Brittney Fraser is a sophomore at Stanford and loving it. Rachel Charity, one of my best friends who joined after we wrote the book, is a freshman at Clemson and is really enjoying the South. Jamexis Christian is a junior at Boston College and just finished spending a semester in London. Jen Green is a sophomore at Hofstra and is majoring in Marketing. Rebecca Chastang just moved back to D.C. from New Jersey and is in her junior year at Brown. Shannon Sanders is a junior, at Spelman along with Nikki Jourdain-Earl who is also a junior and they are both doing great. Maya Yette is a freshman at Wake Forest with a focus on Communications. Ashley Speights is a sophomore at the University of Virginia and recently pledged Delta Gamma. Mariel Fernandez is a sophomore at the University of Chicago. Brittany Lattisaw is currently at Haverford. Holly Thomas is a freshman at McDaniel, majoring in History.

While so much has changed, one of my favorite books is still *The Ear, the Eye, and the Arm* by Nancy Farmer, which was the first book the original Mother-Daughter Book Club read.

What mother doesn't have a secret agenda as we go about plotting good times for our children? The family vacations, the slumber parties, the new diary. Sometimes we yearn to give them what we didn't have at their age. Sometimes we hope to fan an ember of memory into a glow to warm the rest of their lives. No matter what we had in mind, the reality always holds some surprises.

When I first thought of organizing the Mother-Daughter Book Club, I'll admit I had an agenda. It wasn't creating memories that motivated me, although I hoped that would be a benefit. And it wasn't as if I had some soulful longing for literary discussion, though I've always enjoyed the company of women and girls. No, my motivation was planted very firmly in the here and now.

My daughter Morgan had just turned nine years old, and we enjoyed the full range of emotions and dialogue you might expect of two creative, determined females with a generation between them. It seemed we were constantly butting heads over everyday things. More and more, I realized that I needed—and wanted—to find a way to spend some special time with Morgan that would help us understand each other better and give us a close relationship as she grew up.

"I spend time with each of my children, one-on-one, but I like the Mother-Daughter Book Club because it is not just you and the child, but a group of peers and parents all having something in common. And all of us are interested in wanting to build more of a relationship between mother and daughter."

Alice

WHAT IS IT ABOUT GIRLS . . .

Like a lot of other mothers, I was beginning to ask myself: "How do you know what girls are actually thinking about? How do you plant the seeds of the values you want to take hold in their lives if they won't listen to you when you talk to them one-on-one?"

Another mother of a preteen daughter put it this way: "We can be standing on the same square foot of earth, looking up at the same sky, and we still manage to see things differently. We get along fine, but I suspect that when it comes to knowing what she's really thinking about things, the truth is often I don't have a clue."

All of us—mothers and daughters alike—do see things differently. Not only that, we actually *see different things*. It's like what happens at the checkout line at the supermarket when you're waiting there, confronted with tabloids and magazines with headlines that shout about every conceivable angle on life: how to get a man, how to please a man, how to diet, how to dress for success from the boardroom to the bedroom, how to have great sex, how to flatten your stomach, thin your thighs, quit smoking—the headlines go on and on and on. I'm gazing at those covers and not giving them a second thought. I know fact from fiction when it comes to suggestions about my body, my relationships, and my life. But when Morgan, or the girl behind us, reads those covers, what happens to all those lifestyle messages, those images of flawless supermodels and carousing celebrities? Our girls don't need books to be readers. They're reading the world everywhere they go, from the checkout line to the television screen. All day our daughters are gathering images and ideas about the world, about themselves, and about their futures.

As caring mothers, we want to know what they're making of it. Sometimes we do know. Sometimes we just wish we did, maybe with the hope that if we knew what they were thinking we could cheer on the conclusions we like and change the ones we don't. Direct questions don't get you anywhere, either. What does a girl think about the glimpses of life she sees or hears each day in advertising, on television, and in popular music? What does she make of it all?

> "You always have these great goals of doing something special with your child, and then the laundry comes up. Having the structure of the book club seems like a nice way to spend some time with your daughter and her friends and see what they're thinking about."
>
> *Leslye*

"Nothing," shrugs Morgan, then eleven.

I don't believe that. But I do believe that's precisely what most girls would say if you asked them. They *don't* know what they're making of it. As their mothers, we're finding out the hard way—from our own experiences or those of families around us—that the culture imposes harshly on our girls' views of themselves, of us, and of their prospects for the future.

In *Reviving Ophelia: Saving the Selves of Adolescent Girls*, author Mary Pipher, a clinical psychologist, tells us something most of us already know in our hearts:

"In order to keep their true selves and grow into healthy adults, girls need love from family and friends, meaningful work, respect, challenges, and physical and psychological safety. They need identities based on talents or interests rather than appearance, popularity or sexuality. They need good habits for coping with stress, self-nurturing skills and a sense of purpose and perspective. They need quiet places and times. They need to feel that they are part of something larger than their own lives and that they are emotionally connected to the whole."

Other formal studies deliver similar conclusions. Despite some differences in cultural attitudes among girls of different races or ethnic groups, one common theme comes through loud and clear: Life circumstances and the messages girls absorb from their world shape their attitudes about themselves and other girls.

So, if our life circumstances include the scream of high-tech audio-video-electronic cultural influences, how can the calm, purposeful pursuit of books and conversation begin to make a significant difference?

> "In the group, I can be the mom, or the professional, or the 'aunt,' if you will, to the other girls—and they get to see various sides of me—we see different sides of each other, and that is good."
>
> *Alexis*

WHAT IS IT ABOUT BOOKS . . .

Books have always been a refuge, a place where we put aside the routine of the day and step into someone else's story, where we can laugh, cry, gasp, or wonder at the goings-on without being responsible for any of it. The story's success doesn't depend on our wisdom or patience; the main character isn't waiting for us to drive her to dance class or pick up poster board for a homework assignment.

Books are a great equalizer. You may not have the money to travel the world, but with a library card as your passport your horizons for exploration and self-discovery are unlimited.

BOOKS TO GROW ON

Books of undeserved obscurity,
I call them:

The Mouse and His Child
Russell Hoban

The Gammage Cup
Carol Kendall

Drop Dead
Julia Cunningham

Jingo Django
Sid Fleischman

Elidor
Stan Garner

Goody Hall
Natalie Babbitt

—CYNTHIA VOIGT, AUTHOR,
Homecoming

You can visit cultures from around the globe and learn about *anything* that interests you.

Reading can be emotionally freeing as well, as one woman shared with me: "I was a very sick child, alone a lot, and books became my friend," she said. "If you come to a sad place in a book, you can cry and the book doesn't tell you to stop. You can laugh, reading a book, when you might not be able to laugh with other people. If you're shy or sick or just alone, you can experience emotions you couldn't experience any other way."

If you've ever read a book and chatted about it with someone or enjoyed a lively group discussion, then you know that books can be bridges as well. Book talk fills the gentle open spaces of time and distance between friends. It can span generations, and criss-cross the textured geography of differing cultures. It makes a neat, quick plank for conversation with someone new. You don't have to know someone to talk books with them, but when you talk books with someone, you're getting to know them.

When we share the experience of reading with our children, books create a garden, a special sunlit corner where our relationship can grow alongside but apart from the crowded landscape of everyday life.

That's what the Mother-Daughter Book Club is all about. Staking out that special garden space, tending it lightly together, inviting a handful of others to join in, and sharing the harvest of pleasure and discovery. And the growing season never ends!

WHAT IS IT ABOUT LIFE . . .

Our daughters need this growing space. They are partners with us in family life, but as they grow, so does their excitement at the very prospect of growing up and the independence that comes with it. As they search for their own authentic life view, the voice that comes from their own heart, they're listening to the voices all around them: those of family, friends, and teachers, as well as magazine covers, fashion and lifestyle trends, news headlines, and the din of popular culture.

At school—no matter how good the program—they make their way in that tangled wood, on a good day exercising their minds and developing their talents as the culture permits. The forest is thick with the undergrowth of social, emotional, and developmental issues, and it grows thicker as each year progresses.

Academics? In studies conducted by the American Association of University Women, researchers have described the typical school culture as one that teaches our daughters to silence themselves, discounting their learning styles, curbing their questions, and focusing instead upon striving to please.

In short, the confident girl who spoke up with a math answer in September may only occasionally be raising her hand by November and will feign ignorance by December to avoid being branded a "brain."

Even so, the desire for recognition is there and the competition is fierce. Especially as they become increasingly sensitive to boys' reactions, girls may become reluctant to take the intellectual risks—with the potential for failure—that are necessary to build confidence and competence. And the pressure is on whether the girls attend school with boys or with girls only. In their preteen years, girls can become cliquish in the worst ways, imposing social suffering on other girls who differ in any way from the in-group's power brokers that day.

At the end of a long school day, many girls step out the door and into a rush of after-school classes where they pursue their special interests. We juggle car pool duty or on our own get them where they need to go: dance, soccer, music, swimming, drama, art, gymnastics. If

---

BOOKS TO GROW ON

My first memory is *Go, Dog, Go,* the part about the hat. I remember being fascinated by *James and the Giant Peach.*

James and the Giant Peach
Roald Dahl

The Borrowers
Mary Norton

Charlotte's Web
E. B. White

Go, Dog, Go
Philip D. Eastman

Little Women
Louisa May Alcott

—JAMIE LEE CURTIS,
ACTRESS, AUTHOR,
Tell Me Again About the Night I Was Born

---

we see them at all, it's to pump them up with a snack, pop them into a car, and, between traffic lights, practice our gentle art of motherly interrogation to learn something, *anything*, about their day:

"What did you learn today?" I would ask Morgan on the way home from school. Her reply: "I don't know. Stuff."

Direct questions just never get you anywhere.

Evenings are prime time for conversation. But there's housework, homework, and other preparations for tomorrow's return to the hubbub of work and school. Fortunately for me, Morgan was a night owl, and we shared our reading and chat time at an hour when most of her friends were already asleep. After a typical day, most mothers and daughters we know consider the night a success if they can squeeze in time for a hug and a kiss on the way to sleep.

So, how could *another* organized activity—and a group one, at that—be so satisfying and rewarding? I think it's because a mother-daughter book club doesn't *require*, it *invites*. Instead of obligations, it offers enrichment. It takes what we bring to it—a love of reading, lively conversation, and friendship—and amplifies those pleasures. The club format provides just enough structure so we can relax. And into the comfortable familiarity of our circle, it introduces with each book a raft of new characters, with their own ideas and experiences, to broaden our view.

"When they're on their own and it's girls only, there are different dynamics than in a mixed group with boys. There's a lot more honesty, connecting and sharing."
Whitney Ransome,
National Coalition
of Girls' Schools

WHAT IS IT ABOUT A MOTHER-DAUGHTER BOOK CLUB . . .

It doesn't matter if you haven't taken time to read a novel in years. Or if your daughter seems to read only when it's assigned at school. Whether or not you or your daughter is a devoted reader, the Mother-Daughter Book Club works because it isn't just about books. And it isn't just about reading or mastering analytical skills. It's about mothers and daughters, girls and women, and how reading and talking together can enrich our relationships with one another and strengthen our daughters' courage to be themselves.

The benefits are real, and we see them in action not only at our meetings, but in the girls' lives at home, at school, and all around.

THE CLUB ENCOURAGES READING

The girls read because they want to. The club motivates the girls to read. Some love reading anyway. But others read because they want to be prepared for the discussion and any activities planned around the book.

"They're not all girls who like to read and have great analytical skills, but they all are excited about coming to socialize," says Linda Chastang. "For the girl who doesn't like to read so much, if she wants to come to that meeting, she's going to read that book."

The before-and-after snapshots of our girls as readers provide some convincing evidence:

"Prior to the Mother-Daughter Book Club, Tiffany's only craving for books was *Goosebumps*," says Winnie Donaldson. "I was glad she was reading anything. But over the past year, the club has encouraged her to want to read other books. She's become a more serious reader. It truly is important to her that she reads the book club book so she'll be prepared to participate in discussion at the meetings."

The girls' approach to reading changes and improves, too, we've noticed.

"She's become a very active reader," says Grace Speights, about her daughter, Ashley. "She'll stop and say something like. 'That's stupid,' or 'Why did that character do that?' and she'll ask about similes or metaphors she doesn't understand. She really asks questions. And I can tell she enjoys it because she'll ask, 'Are we going to read tonight?' and she'll be standing there with the book in hand."

> "Maya and her friends were beginning to have more frequent 'whispered conversations.' Reading the same books has helped us to have more in common as she approaches the age when children begin to distance themselves from their parents."
>
> *Joyce*

CRITICAL THINKING SKILLS GET A WORKOUT

Through discussions of the plots, characters, and authors' writing styles, the girls are learning how to take an idea and pull it apart to see what makes it tick, build on it, question it, find evidence to support their opinion of it, and use that experience to reflect in greater depth on their own lives or the lives of others.

"These kids are really reading these books and connecting things," says Leslye Fraser. "They'll say things like, 'I'd give it an 8.5,' and they'll analyze the good and the bad, and they'll say the author should have done this or that. It's been nice watching

BOOKS TO GROW ON

This is a list of books from my childhood, which was a long time ago, since I am now ninety. Today's children, it seems to me, are missing so much not reading more folk and fairy tales.

English Fairy Tales and *More English Fairy Tales*
Joseph Jacobs

Grimms' Fairy Tales
Jacob and Wilhelm Grimm

Blue Fairy Book and *Red Fairy Book*
Andrew Lang

Heidi
Johanna Spyri

The Secret Garden
Frances Hodgson Burnett

Little Women
Louisa May Alcott

Jane Eyre
Charlotte Brontë

Dandelion Cottage
Carroll Watson Rankin

Downright Dencey
Caroline Dale Sneder

—BEVERLY CLEARY, AUTHOR,
Ramona the Pest

them be in charge, assuming the leadership role with no problem, no fear. And they encourage each other."

It seems like we each see a success story unfolding in our daughter's life.

Alice Thomas recalls how impressed she was the first time she heard her daughter, Holly, hold forth on the book of the day: "I knew she was getting the story okay, but when we got to the meeting and I heard her talking about all these details in the story, and tying them together to make a statement about the character, I was just amazed—I had no idea she was thinking that deeply about it—and I was proud."

These girls, who can't remember to close the door on their way out, nonetheless remember intricate details of plots and characters that pass through our discussion circle:

"I'm always pleasantly surprised at how girls compare characters from book to book, or reflect on different writing styles," says Joyce Yette. "Maybe I should get used to the fact that they're bright and curious, but I wouldn't have imagined these kinds of discussions."

A FRIENDLY FORUM FOR DISCUSSING IMPORTANT ISSUES

By talking about the impersonal—plots, characters, and author's choices—we've heard the girls' candid thoughts on important issues like death and illness, friendship and marriage, family relationships and school and social issues.

"What's been nice is gaining some insight into how they think," Leslye says. "We sometimes take for granted that our children share our life experience—for instance, some of the unhappy things we could all remember from our childhoods—but their comments make it clear that those experiences aren't necessarily part of their lives. That has been a pleasant surprise."

"Some of the issues in the books have been a little delicate, but we talk about them anyway," says Alexis Christian. "If we don't talk about it, who else will? Who do we want the girls to talk about sensitive issues with, if not us?"

A CHANCE TO SEE FRIENDS, MAKE FRIENDS OUTSIDE SCHOOL

The smaller group size and the emotional comfort level of a mother-daughter book club makes it a safe, supportive place for a girl to venture outside the lines she draws for herself each day at school. The combination of laughter, play, and talk creates a natural habitat for learning within a circle of caring mothers.

"It gives the girls an opportunity to discuss books without being under pressure like they are at school, wondering if this is the answer the teacher is looking for," says Kathie Thompson. "In our book club there are no right or wrong answers. You can say what you feel."

Even the girls who are a bit shy, who typically might be reluctant to say what they feel, are finding a voice in our circle.

"This close, supportive setting has provided an excellent opportunity for Maya, who has always been so shy and quiet, to express herself," says her mom, Joyce. "With each meeting, her voice has become a little louder, her eye contact has become a little more direct, and her confidence has grown a little stronger."

Morgan likes the speak-up-and-be-heard atmosphere, too. Says she: "It's much easier than school because you're not writing; you're just talking. A lot of the kids in the club like to talk a lot, so it's nice because that's what we're *supposed* to do!"

STRENGTHENS THE MOTHER-DAUGHTER RELATIONSHIP

Relationships are built on understanding, and this is an easy, gentle way to gain understanding. There are very few regular opportunities in our lives to relax and enjoy one another's company and express our feelings or ideas about what goes on in the world without lecturing.

"One thing I like is that we're able to look at things from a different perspective and try to start helping them think from a different perspective," says Cheryl Brown. "Often the way we phrase our questions is deliberately done so we generate some new thoughts. You don't want to provide answers for the girls, but kind of help them see it differently. A mother can rephrase things, pull ideas out and focus on them, and ask some thought-provoking questions."

Whatever our differences in perspective, the time we share talking at meetings and at home brings us closer to our daughters in ways that feel right.

"The relationship between mothers and daughters in those teen years can get a little strained," Alexis says, "but at this stage, it's a wonderful opportunity for me to actually sit down with Jamexis, even a chance to touch her—stroke her hair, make sure she's okay—it's some real time we can share and be best friends because women can become best friends, and hopefully she'll understand she can tell me anything because I plan to tell her everything."

We all share that desire for emotional closeness with our children, and the challenge of creating ways for it to grow.

"It's difficult, because in the normal flow of the parent-child relationship at this age the parent is viewed as the authoritarian who will be angry or upset if you say something wrong," Grace says. "It's hard for them to cross the line—they're thinking, 'This is my mom, but she's also my friend,' and until you have some kind of relationship where you can show that side in a natural way, it's a hard thing to do. This gives us a chance to do that. I want Ashley to view me as a mom who is open and willing to talk about anything that she wants to talk about, no matter what the subject."

> "The funniest thing that happened at a meeting was when we discussed the folk tales in *Her Stories* by Virginia Hamilton, and our moms asked us to describe the man that we would like to marry. Although we had all been very talkative at every meeting, this question from the moms just caused us to giggle."
>
> *Ashley S.*

A WHOLESOME FEELING OF BELONGING

Along with the fun, the group provides affirmation—a feeling of recognition and acceptance—that our adolescent girls need. A story I heard one evening at a Girl Scout board meeting left me and a room full of others in tears, and it tells me we're right to be concerned and we're on the right track with our book discussion club. The speaker told us of a letter she had received from a college girl—a former Girl Scout. The young woman had written that she was sitting at her desk at 3 a.m., her roommate in the throes of an emotional crisis, feelings of despair thick in the dormitory room. She wrote about the emotional tempests of college life, but added that she was keeping an even keel, and concluded that it was her experience as a Girl Scout that had given her a strong, sure belief in herself. There really are very few places where girls get that message of affirmation in a continuing way. Our Mother-Daughter Book Club does that for our daughters.

The Mother-Daughter Book Club provides a kind of balance to the life our girls experience at school and the view they see of mothers at home or at work. They even experience *each other* differently than they do in other settings.

"We don't all go to the same school and see each other every day, so when we get together, it's like a party, and you play and play until it's time to go home," says Holly Thomas, ten. "The book discussion is fun, so it's like part of the party."

"It's really nice if you like reading *and* if you want to make more friends *and* if you want to get to know people better," says Maya Yette, ten. "It's fun to get to play at other people's houses more."

"It gives you the chance to talk about the books so you're not just reading them and putting them down. You're really understanding."
        Maya

Those simple thoughts ring true. Even the girls who knew one another well have seen their relationships flower around our meeting discussions.

"My favorite part of the book club meetings is the social part, when we eat and talk and play games," says Rebecca Chastang, eleven. "The books are okay, too."

Our reading, meetings, and discussion allow our girls the freedom to focus on:

📖 SHARING INSTEAD OF COMPETITION: There's eagerness in the discussion but never a race to see who can "win" the race to give a right answer. "In school, there's always a right and wrong answer, so usually I don't answer if I think I might get it wrong,'" says Brittney Fraser, ten. "This was new to me—I was nervous at first because I thought everybody was going to say 'No!' like they do in class. But they didn't."

📖 REFLECTION INSTEAD OF PERFORMANCE: By posing questions that draw on the girls' experience as well as their understanding of a story, the discussion invites thought and comment. It encourages reflection, because the more thought you put into an answer, the more everyone responds to it, and that's an immediate source of enjoyment for everyone. "When we read the book *The Friends* by Rosa Guy, I liked that book," says Ashley Brown, twelve. "The fact that it talks about friendship and how there are problems sometimes, but you can work things out. It made me think about my friends."

📖 ACCEPTANCE INSTEAD OF JUDGMENT: Discussion offers a safe haven for expression. Since every perspective is valuable in an open discussion, each person's comments receive the same respect and acknowledgment. Some comments lead to more vigorous discussion than others, but it's not because the comment is good or bad. It's the chemistry of the moment, and the girls quickly become comfortable in that judgment-free zone. "I never knew it was so easy to express your opinions," says Ashley Speights, ten. "I used to be very shy about that, but now it doesn't seem so hard to say what I think about something."

📖 **EXPLORATION INSTEAD OF MASTERY:** The shy one can speak without fear of ridicule, and the perfectionist learns to share her full rainbow of ideas instead of narrowing her contributions to just "the right answer." The careful exploration of ideas helps girls develop a sense of mastery, a comfort level with critical thinking skills that they need to hold their own in other circles or circumstances. "When we're all talking about the same book, some people have different ideas and it opens up a new perspective you didn't even think about, and then you listen and understand it." says Jamexis Christian, twelve.

📖 **EXPERIENCE INSTEAD OF OBJECTIVES:** In most other realms of our lives we face a constant pressure to achieve results: meet deadlines, make good grades, meet expectations of our own or of others. You can't make an A in the Mother-Daughter Book Club: There is no performance review. The experience is what there is, all there is, and it is the experience that teaches us the most about the books and about ourselves. "Discussing the book is my favorite part of the meeting," says Jihan Thompson, twelve. "Sometimes the mothers might bring up a topic, and people will say how they feel about it or give their views on the book. It's really fun to get different people's insights on it."

📖 **SEEING MOTHERS AS INDIVIDUALS INSTEAD OF EXPERTS OR MANAGERS:** Mothers enjoy the same respectful treatment as every member of the discussion group, and that sense of equality in this setting allows our girls to see us more as individuals, as interesting women with thoughts to share. Here, our years of life experience don't make us "boss." Our experience only adds to the richness of the conversation.

It didn't take Morgan long to warm up to some real conversation. "At our very first meeting, some of us weren't so

BOOKS TO GROW ON

Some of these came from my "Women Writing in French"
course. Others came from my work on women and girls and
general reading.

So Long a Letter
Manama Ba

Mother to Daughter, Daughter to Mother
edited by Tillie Olsen

*Meeting at the Crossroads: Women's Psychology
and Girls' Development*
Lyn Mikel Brown and Carol Gilligan

The Book of the City of Ladies
Christine de Pizan

The Lais of Marie de France
Marie de France

Women's Friendships: A Collection of Short Stories,
edited by Susan Koppelman

Between Mothers and Daughters: Stories Across a Generation,
edited by Susan Koppelman

—ELLEN SILBER,
Director of the Marymount Institute for
the Education of Women and Girls

used to doing things like this with our moms, but once we got started talking, it just started flowing and then it was just great," Morgan says. "Now it's always that way."

The fact that we're all so busy, mothers and daughters alike, makes it a special experience when we simply sit down in a place together to talk—instead of *to get something done*.

"I have homework, and she has work and Girl Scouts," says Tiffany Donaldson, eleven, whose mother, Winnie, is a Girl Scout leader, among other things. "When I'm home, I'm reading or working on homework and she's doing Girl Scouts and other stuff, so I pretty much don't get to talk to her. I like hearing her ideas about our books at the meetings."

What's in it for us, the mothers? Some of the benefits are those we had in mind when we started—dreams come true:

📖 We express ourselves as individuals, beyond our roles in the family, community, or workplace.

📖 We treasure this special time with our daughters outside the flurry of family life.

📖 We enjoy the company of women and girls with a similar interest in exploring literature and the world of ideas and intellectual exchange. "As we explore places we probably will never visit, talk about things that probably would not come up in the ordinary course of our lives, get to know characters unlike any we'd ever meet, and share our thoughts and experiences with other mothers and their daughters," Linda says, "we have grown closer and we have learned a lot about each other—how alike and different we are, and how much we learn from each other."

Beyond those gifts was a surprise that I never anticipated that day I took my quiet agenda of hope and put it into action: the experience of discovering *myself,* the *woman* at the heart of the mother, daughter, wife, sister, colleague, and friend that I am to others. Through reading and chatting with Morgan, and exploring our stories together with the women and girls in our group, it's as if we're picking up our threads of experience, some old, some new, and weaving them into the fabric of our lives today. It is a comfortable cloth, with texture and color, and it has the feel of truth.

A mother-daughter book club gives you and your daughter the space in your relationship and your schedules to do all this, and you don't have to be an "expert" to make it happen. You don't need a college degree in literature, and your daughter doesn't have to get A's in reading at school to enjoy a mother-daughter book club. You've already got all you need: a desire to spend some quality time with your daughter and a willingness to do something about it!

ENDNOTES

Literature and discussion can strengthen the bond between mothers and daughters.

> "My mom and I can also discuss the books outside of the meetings, which helps us learn about each other in ways we might not otherwise. I share a new bond with my mom due to the book club and the discussions and ideas that come out of it."
>
> *Brooke*

"It has helped me because we can relate to one another better. Now we have all these little things to discuss and argue about. The material from book club gives us an outlet, a chance to sit down and focus so we don't have to be worrying about all those little things."

Sylvie

📖 A mother–daughter book club encourages reading.

"Being in a book club has pushed me to read books I would not otherwise read, and I am glad."

Riley

"Until our mother-daughter book club read *The Curious Incident of the Dog in the Night-time* by Marc Haddon, I would have never known I had an interest in mysteries."

Celia

📖 The reading club format gives girls a chance to develop critical thinking skills outside the classroom.

📖 An intimate circle of mothers, daughters, and friends provides a sense of affirmation and a place to be heard.

"I actually enjoy talking in big groups of people and letting my ideas be heard."

Jesse

"I feel so comfortable talking about books with our book club because I know the people around me genuinely care what I have to say."

Hannah

TWO

How to Organize Your Book Club

THE READING AND DISCUSSION GROUP IS AS ENDURING AS THE WRITTEN WORD, FOR AS LONG AS WORDS HAVE BEEN WRITTEN, PEOPLE HAVE READ, CONTEMPLATED AND GATHERED TO TALK ABOUT THEM.

—ALAN MOORES, RHEA RUBIN
"Let's Talk About It," American Library Association

Skylar Fykes & Shireen Dodson

Hi, my name is Skylar Shireen Fykes. I'm fifteen and a sophomore at Georgetown Day School in Washington, D.C. I have a sister, Morgan, who is twenty. Everyone says we look just alike, but I don't see the resemblance at all. I also have a brother named Leroy, who is twenty-five. I enjoy being the youngest because I have been able to learn from my older siblings' mistakes.

I don't have a favorite book. I have read so many books that I love that I cannot choose one to call my favorite. There are also too many different kinds of books, "magical" books as opposed to books about real people in real situations. When it comes to "magical" books, I loved the Harry Potter books (I was one of those crazy kids lined up at midnight to see the movie, too); I also loved *The Golden Compass, The Subtle Knife,* and *The Amber Spyglass* by Philip Pullman. I also like "trashy" books like the Gossip Girl series and *The A-List* by Zoey Dean. I loved *The Sisterhood of the Traveling Pants.*

Most of the time the books that I read inspire me to do things I wouldn't have done otherwise. For example, I might be tempted to try foods or music mentioned in the book. *The Sisterhood of the Traveling Pants* inspired me to create traveling pants with two of my best friends from camp. We met at debate camp over the summer at Stanford University and we were really sad about leaving each other. We collectively came up with the pants idea. The pants were Hadley's, who lives in Missouri. The third sister is Audrey, who lives in California. Every month, we mail the pants to each other along with letters of what happened while we were wearing the pants. But unlike the book we do wash the pants! It's our way of keeping in touch with each other.

I am active in organizations inside and outside of school. In school I am in Black Culture Club, Young Women of Color, Step

Team, Monday Night Tutoring, Rapture (a gospel singing group), Debate Team, and I take photos for the *Augar Bit*, my school newspaper. I also play varsity soccer and track. Outside of school I am in Jack and Jill, where I am the co-head of the community service group.

My favorite groups are the Step Team, Rapture, and soccer. I love performing more than anything. It gives me such a rush when I am on stage stepping or singing. There is nothing comparable to the feeling you get when the crowd goes wild. There is a similar feeling when I score a goal in a soccer game and the adrenaline is pumping. I love any type of competition because I am a very competitive person.

I love eating and shopping. I love all types of food. It's all amazing. There must be four billion different ways to cook chicken, and before I die I want to try them all. I love shopping because who doesn't? I love bargains. A $100 pair of shoes on sale for $30. Yes! It just doesn't get any better than that. Also who doesn't love a good party? It's amazing when friends get together to hang out, dance, eat, sing, watch a movie, cry. It's all good.

My mom is Shireen Dodson. As you have already read, she is the mom behind the whole mother-daughter book club movement. My middle name is my mom's first name, which is pretty cool because Shireen is a pretty name. My mom and I disagree a lot on what I am allowed to do, but it has gotten better since the beginning of the mother-daughter book club. It's easier to talk to her now because I have a better understanding of some of the things that she has been through as a person. My mom and dad have just recently separated so we have been spending more and more time together. I'm not going to lie; it has been frustrating especially when articles like "The Secret Life of Teens" come out in a local magazine and my mom wants to talk about the same issues over and over again. But I must admit usually after we have a discussion about the issue at hand we have reinforced another layer of trust.

I f you've ever planned a birthday party, you can organize a mother-daughter book club.

I don't mean to make it sound overly easy. It does take some careful thought and planning. But organizing a book club is actually simpler than the administrative job most of us do each week to juggle everyone's schedules

> "The books are long and they're boring in the beginning. But they get interesting in the middle and the end."
>
> *Brittney*

and expectations. And there are some very nice differences: First, the organizing task itself is something enjoyable to do with your daughter. And second, unlike the cluttered closets, family meals, or after-school activity schedule, your book club needs to be organized only once!

It helps to think about your Mother-Daughter Book Club in its essential terms right from the start. What is "the most important thing" about your club? What do you want it to accomplish?

My reasons for wanting to start a book discussion club were fairly straightforward. I saw a mother-daughter book club as a way to spend some special time with Morgan, doing something that would get us talking and listening to each other and enjoying the company of other mothers and daughters with similar reading interests. Surprisingly, ten years later, my reasons for starting a club with my second daughter would be exactly the same.

Think about your reasons. Whatever they are, it's important that you keep them in mind as you organize your club, inviting members, establishing meeting times, compiling a book list from which the girls will choose their selections. Each of these choices will influence the personality of your club and the direction it takes over time. Each step deserves some careful thought.

YOUR MOTHER-DAUGHTER PARTNERSHIP: READY, SET . . .

First impressions are important. The way you introduce the idea of the mother-daughter book club to your daughter may make or break your case, so think about the best way to present it to get the response you want—that excited "yes!"

We all bring more enthusiasm to things when we feel we've made a choice to be involved. The partnership you need with your daughter to start a mother-daughter book club will work only if your daughter wants to do it. If your daughter routinely rejoices at your suggestions for how she should spend her free time, then consider yourself indeed blessed and carry on. If, however, your daughter routinely or even occasionally

> "Nobody ever says, 'That's dumb.' The moms and girls encourage each other."
>
> *Joyce*

resists activities you request, or even those you simply suggest, then don't do either. Try wondering out loud. In politics, they call it "floating a trial balloon." To test a potentially controversial idea at a safe distance from any negative fallout, politicians will see to it that somebody leaks the idea to the media. If it gets a positive response, they run up to claim it and carry it forward. If it gets a negative response, they listen from a distance and use the criticism to guide them as they modify the idea for a more successful introduction.

For mothers, that process boils down to one step: Choose

words that make it easy for your daughter to say yes. If your experience is anything like mine, that means making an idea attractive to your daughter, never mind all the reasons that make it an attractive idea to you.

For example, here are two different ways to suggest to your daughter that you two start a mother-daughter book club. As you read them, imagine your daughter's reaction:

STYLE # 1
Mother: "I've got a great idea. Let's start a mother-daughter book club. We can assign books that are better literature than those paperbacks you read all the time. It'll give us all a chance to talk about the really important issues in life. And when you hear the other mothers' opinions, you'll see I'm not the only one who thinks the way I do."

I can hear the footsteps fade as she runs in the other direction.

STYLE # 2
Mother: "What would you think of inviting a group of your friends and their moms to read books, and then have a get-together with refreshments where you girls could relax and we'd all get to share what we thought about the story and do some fun activity with it?"

Style #2 was my choice, and Morgan took off running—to get the pencil and paper to make her list and start her invitations.

"I thought it was a good idea because usually you don't get to spend a lot of time with your mom, so I liked having something where I could spend time with my mom and with my friends." Morgan says.

What if your daughter hands you a negative response even with a positive introduction? She wouldn't be the first skeptic in the crowd.

"I thought, 'Oh no, here goes another thing,'" recalls Brittney. "I thought piano was going to be fun, and it turned out not to be. I thought basketball was going to be fun, and it turned out not to be. I thought soccer and softball were going to be fun, and they weren't. And I thought swimming was supposed to be fun, and it turned out to be quite boring. So I thought, 'Oh no, another thing I have to go to.'"

If your daughter balks, find out why. Listen to her reasons. You may discover that she doesn't understand the idea or thinks it would be more challenging or demanding than it really is. You may discover that she has personal reservations about reading or about socializing that deserve your attention. You both may discover that through talking about her response, you can identify the parts of the idea that *do* sound exciting, and use those to define the terms for your mother-daughter book club. If she really seems opposed to the idea, then drop it! Suggest the idea to another mother, and see if your daughter changes her mind when she gets an invitation in the mail to join her friends.

> "Our Mother-Daughter Book Club has been everything I thought it might be, and maybe a little more, because I didn't imagine in the beginning that the girls would bring about the depth of discussion that they have."
>
> *Alice*

My point here is not to tell you how to talk with your

daughter but to suggest that our efforts to communicate with our daughters work best when we try to see the moment through their eyes. That's a big part of what the Mother-Daughter Book Club is about—listening to our girls and truly sharing the experience instead of directing it. As a woman and mother with a take-charge habit, it has taken me some time, and practice, to learn when to hit my pause button and listen: *listen* to my daughter's words and, with a caring heart, *hear* what she is saying.

Once the idea has the unanimous approval of the two of you, it's time to find some good company.

GIRL BY GIRL, MOM BY MOM: BUILDING A DISCUSSION GROUP

We're always instructing our girls to be inclusive, to keep the circle open as they play at recess or after school, or as they make their way through life. And I bristle when I hear about girls and cliques at school, or remember them from my own girlhood.

So when Morgan and I sat down to discuss whom to invite to be in our Mother-Daughter Book Club, the fact that we were "picking" people seemed right and wrong at the same time. Why not invite all of Morgan's closest friends? Why not include those mothers with whom I had a close friendship, even if the girls weren't particularly close? Our "open door" policy had always served us well in the past. Why select a group now?

For the answer, go back to your original reasons for wanting to start a mother-daughter book club. For us, one of my motivations was the thought that this group would give Morgan and me an opportunity to spend time with each other and some friends we didn't see very often, exploring a common element of

BOOKS TO GROW ON

I've simply selected books that I enjoyed reading at the time
and that I find returning to my thoughts again and again.
All of the books are thought-provoking and should be great
discussion books. They range from serious to whimsical, from
fact to fantasy. Although *Mrs. Mike*, published in 1947, may
seem a bit out of place, I had to include it as it was my favorite
book as a young girl. I first read it when I was in sixth grade
and continued to read it at least once a year well into college.

Mrs. Mike
Benedict Freedman

The Giver
Lois Lowry

The Man from the Other Side
Uri Orlev

Dealing with Dragons
Patricia C. Wrede

Louisa May: The World and Works of Louisa May Alcott
Norma Johnston

Grace
Jill Paton Walsh

The Bomb
Theodore Taylor

Running Out of Time
Margaret Peterson Haddix

—BARBARA J. MCKILLIP,
FOUNDER AND PRESIDENT,
The Libri Foundation

our lives—our African American heritage. At first we planned to focus completely on books by African American authors or about the black experience. Our reading selections quickly expanded beyond that original idea, to reflect our full range of interests. But the composition of the group—all African American mothers and daughters—has become a wonderful source of support and experience of our cultural heritage, a theme that is missing from the girls' school programs and extracurricular activities, where they most often are a small racial minority.

> **BOOKS TO GROW ON**
>
> These are books from my childhood that I still love to read:
>
> *The Bible*
>
> *Winnie the Pooh*
> A. A. Milne
>
> *The Secret Garden*
> Frances Hodgson Burnett
>
> *The Yearling*
> Marjorie Kinnan Rawlings
>
> *A Tale of Two Cities*
> Charles Dickens
>
> —KATHERINE PATERSON, AUTHOR,
> *Bridge to Terabithia*

Whatever your vision for the group, whether you plan to invite only girls and mothers you know well or post your invitation on a library or Sunday school bulletin board for an open enrollment, you're hoping that the individuals who respond will be a "good fit." That doesn't mean they should all think alike. It does mean that they need to share the vision or goals you have for your group; they should be able to participate in the group's reading, discussion, and activities in a meaningful way, and they should be able to follow through on any commitment they make to host or help coordinate the group meetings.

Some qualities that contribute to a "good fit" include:

📖 An interest in reading

📖 Reading skill level that makes reading a pleasurable activity

📖 Age or grade level close to the others

📖 Maturity level in the range necessary to participate fully in the reading, discussion, and related activities

📖 Comfort in discussion

📖 A cooperative attitude

📖 An acquaintance or friendship with others in the group

📖 An interesting mix of viewpoints for the mothers, including differences of opinion shaped by each woman's life experience. It's best if every mother can be up-front about any personal sensitivities—religious, political, or otherwise—that would influence her enjoyment of the group or otherwise affect the group.

📖 If you want to create a group that shares a special interest or objective, think of girls who bring that particular life experience or reading interest to the group. (See Chapter Nine: "Using Themes to Guide Choices.")

This process of selecting whom to invite is an opportunity to help your daughter learn about team building. They get plenty of experience in team*work* in their other school and after-school activities: cooperative learning projects at school, dance class, soccer teams, Girl Scouts. All of them offer wonderful opportunities for girls to gather together and experience the challenges and delights of playing, performing, or working toward a goal in a cooperative way.

BOOKS TO GROW ON

Over the years there have been a number of books that my daughters and I have enjoyed. The following is a list of some of our favorites:

Little Women
Louisa May Alcott

Anne Frank: The Diary of a Young Girl
Anne Frank

Charlotte's Web
E. B. White

The Nancy Drew series
Carolyn Keene

Little House on the Prairie
Laura Ingalls Wilder

I also recommend the biographies of such influential women as Eleanor Roosevelt, Olympic legend Wilma Rudolph, and Susan B. Anthony, and also the writings of Maya Angelou. The lives of these women can serve as a source of inspiration to us all.

—TIPPER GORE

Team *building* is different. It requires that you think about your goal and think about the qualities needed for the team to work well. In terms of a mother-daughter book club, it's important to aim for a lively yet harmonious blend of personalities and talents. All of our friends have special qualities. It's a matter of thinking about them, and tapping those girls and mothers who seem most likely to enjoy and enable others to enjoy good books, relaxed socializing, and stimulating discussion.

This is another opportunity to listen to our daughters and show some trust, be willing to take a chance on their judgment. Morgan was absolutely determined that one of her younger friends—an eight-year-old girl who was not an avid reader—be invited to join the group. I resisted at first, believing that she simply wasn't quite ready to participate in a book discussion group. As it turned out, the mother and daughter were so enthusiastic about the idea that both were willing to put in extra effort to tackle the challenging reading assignments. And the perspectives and creativity they have brought to the group are cherished. Morgan *knew;* I listened and learned.

THE MORE THE MERRIER . . . UP TO A POINT

When you've got your list of names ready, it's time to do a little simple math. How many girls and mothers should you invite to establish your club?

I can share the advice of experts: The Great Books Foundation, in its suggestions for organizing book discussion groups for young people, suggests starting with eight to ten children. Teachers have recommended that from six to ten or so children makes a group small enough to be comfortable yet large enough to keep a discussion going strong.

> "Our mother-daughter book club discussions allowed Jessica to see that she was not alone in coping with a mother with a laundry list of rules and values."
>
> *Sandra*

I happen to be at ease with large groups, especially a group of girls and women I already know. Even so, when Morgan's list topped out at twenty girls, we managed to whittle it to a more realistic twelve invitations that went out in the next day's mail. One of the mothers in our group has told

> "Raising teens isn't a snap, so sharing the experience with others is a great comfort and support."
>
> *Maria*

me since that when she first heard that invitations had gone out to that many girls, she had second thoughts about joining. Her daughter was one of the youngest in the group, a little shy, and not an avid recreational reader. And the thought of eventually hosting a club meeting that brought twenty-four girls and moms into her home was daunting. Still, she and her daughter came for that first meeting and were pleasantly surprised to find that the number of mothers and daughters who actually signed on was quite comfortable.

While you're thinking about numbers, think again about the vision you have for your club. If having the club meet at members' homes is important to you, then you'll need to aim for a number that fits comfortably into your home settings.

For us, meeting at homes was important because it was where we felt we could most completely relax, reflect, and enjoy our discussion. Over time, we also have come to realize that, for us, sharing our homes has been a way of sharing ourselves, and it gives the girls, especially, a tangible feeling of ownership of the club when they host a meeting. When one of our members felt her town house couldn't handle the crowd comfortably, she asked a friend for the use of *her* home. The request was graciously granted.

The ideal number will be small enough to fit comfortably into your meeting place and large enough to sustain a lively discussion even when a few are absent. I suggest inviting about four more girls than the minimum you would hope to have at every meeting. Then if someone misses, or one drops out, you still have a strong core group to keep your club going.

SAMPLE INVITATION

Shireen and Her Daughter Morgan
Invite You to the
Organizing Meeting of the
Mother-Daughter Book Club

Sunday, October 1, 1995

TIME: 4 to 6 P.M.

PLACE: Home of Alexis and Jamexis Christian

RSVP: Shireen or Morgan Fykes

Please bring book ideas and your calendar!

While a written invitation is always nice, the girls say it travels by snail mail. These days e-mail invitations work well, and once the club has settled into a routine date and time a quick e-mail highlighting the meeting location and the book serves as a welcome reminder.

SAMPLE E-MAIL INVITATION

Greetings,

Our Girls have gotten together and the word is they want to start a **Mother-Daughter Book Club.** Skylar and I will host the first meeting. We hope we can count you in on what is sure to be a wonderful journey. So read our book selection (*Whirligig* by Paul Fleischman) and then come on over on **Sunday, March 13, 2005 @ 4:00 P.M.**

Shireen

TAKING THE LEAD: HOW MUCH SHOULD YOU PLAN IN ADVANCE?

When I organize something, I don't like to leave much to chance. So before we sent out our invitations, I called several mothers to be sure they were interested in doing this with us. We talked about the kinds of books we thought would be on-target for our group. And we agreed upon a convenient date for our organizational meeting.

From the moment I knew we were going to do this club, I began scouting the bookstores for books the group might want to read. I must have read fifteen or twenty books in my search for the eight that eventually were introduced to the girls. (See Chapter Four: "How to Find and Read Books.") But my efforts as a previewer paid off for the group. By the time we met for our organizational meeting, we had a good array of books from which the girls could pick one to start, and that made their selection process fairly simple.

There are other ways to blaze the trail to your first meeting and book selection. You might pick the first book yourself and include a copy of it—or simply name it—in the invitation that goes out to your charter members. Then, at your organizational meeting, the group can enjoy its first "official" mother-daughter book discussion.

Every book discussion group is bound to be unique, reflecting the age of its members, their interests, and their life experiences. But our hunt for good books begins at the same place and leads us in the same direction. A wonderful thing— another pleasant surprise—comes out of the process of organizing, of looking for books, reading them, and thinking about the girls, the mother-daughter relationship, the club, the stories and the discussions to come. It becomes absolutely clear that in the hubbub of all this living and literature, a mother-daughter book club is a *right* idea, one that brings us heart to heart, and the prospect of that first meeting becomes truly exciting.

BOOKS TO GROW ON

Ten of my favorite books when I was ten years old:

The Wizard of Oz, L. Frank Baum

Baby Island, Carol Ryrie Brink

Caddie Woodlawn, Carol Ryrie Brink

The Secret Garden, Frances Hodgson Burnett

Understood Betsy, Dorothy Canfield

James and the Giant Peach, Roald Dahl

The Peterkin Papers, Lucretia P. Hale

Misty of Chincoteague, Marguerite Henry

Mary Poppins, P. L. Travers

Stuart Little, E. B. White

Ten books I would now recommend to ten-year-olds:

Sounder, William H. Armstrong

The Secret Garden, Frances Hodgson Burnett

Ramona the Pest, Beverly Cleary

James and the Giant Peach, Roald Dahl

Anne Frank: The Diary of a Young Girl, Anne Frank

A Wrinkle in Time, Madeleine L'Engle

Rascal, Sterling North

Bridge to Terabithia, Katherine Paterson

Roll of Thunder, Hear My Cry, Mildred Taylor

Stuart Little, E. B. White

—ANN MARTIN, AUTHOR,
The Baby-sitters Club series

ENDNOTES

📖 Stay focused on your reasons for starting a mother-daughter book club.

> "The chance to share a laugh, hear a confession, argue a not-quite-cogent perspective, compliment a new haircut, all grist of friendship and belonging, this is the foundation of who we are, my daughter and I. A Sunday afternoon gabbing with the girls? Perfect."
>
> *Pam*

📖 Present the idea of a mother-daughter book club to your daughter as fun.

> "We find ourselves laughing a lot and having a good time. Sometimes someone will recall a story in one of the discussions that makes people laugh. Also the girls always laugh a lot when we do our art project or something like that after the meeting."
>
> *Brooke*

> "It is great to share a common activity with Sylvie. 'Have you read the book yet?' 'Where did you put it?' 'You had it last.' Just the mundane interchanges are fun because they have us relating more as equals than as mother-daughter."
>
> *Kris*

📖 Choose members who share your vision and goals for the club.

> "Make sure that the participants come together because of a love of reading. While the club offers the opportunity to socialize and make new friends, it will fall apart if the girls don't primarily share the love of good books."
>
> *Sandra*

> "The hardest part about forming a club is picking the right members. Once you do that, the rest is easy. The chemistry is really what will hold the group together."
>
> *Morgan*

> "The most difficult and important part of a book club: You have to make sure to pick a group of mothers and daughters that flow through discussions. The challenge is making sure everyone feels comfortable and no one feels overpowered."
>
> *Skylar*

BOOK LOVERS BRAINSTORM
To the Books and Beyond!

- GO GLOBETROTTING! Use a globe to locate the story's setting.

- SEE THE SITES! Check with the local librarian or historical society to find out if any book-related sites might be within traveling distance for your group. Consider having your meeting at the site or planning the field trip for a day of its own.

- WRITE TO AN AUTHOR—Ask your neighborhood librarian for help in locating an address for the author of a book the club has enjoyed. Ask for a volunteer from among the girls to write the club's letter to the author, sharing the group's thoughts about the book and inviting the author to write back if possible.

- COOK OR SERVE FOOD that reflects the era or ethnic flavor of the story, or use a recipe from the book.

- MAKE A STORY-RELATED CRAFT—Try to use materials and tools they would have used at the time in the story.

- LIGHTS! ACTION! READER'S THEATER! No need to memorize—just act out a few favorite scenes using the book as your script. Take turns being the audience and the actors.

- DRESS UP! Come dressed in clothing reminiscent of the era.

- PAPER DOLLS—Make story-related paper dolls from poster board and draw your own outfits to cut out from plain paper.

- STORY SHEETS—Use 3M's poster-sized Post-it sheets to jot down the group's ideas or invite girls to draw characters or scenes to display temporarily on a wall.

• ADJECTIVE AMBUSH—Divide into two teams to see who can find the largest number of descriptive words first to reach a target number. Write down words and page numbers on which they appear in case the challengers call a bluff!

• VERB VENDETTA—Go after the action words now—remember each word has to be found in the book!

• WONDERFUL WORDS—Keep an ongoing collection of great words or phrases the girls circle during home reading and contribute at meeting. Under a heading of the book's title and discussion date, invite each contributor to write her words in the club's book herself.

• PERSONALITY PARADE—Examine characters' personalities—list and discuss their positive and negative qualities.

• TABLETOP THEMES—Create a centerpiece or table decoration that goes along with the story. The host daughter might like to use toys or items she has—dolls, miniature figurines, action figures—to set up a scene from the book.

• BOOKMARKS—Make bookmarks as a memento of a story. Invite each girl to draw a picture of a character or scene from the story on one side of the paper, and on the other side write the name of the book and month and year she read it. Laminate it or use clear adhesive-backed shelf paper to cover the bookmark.

• BOOKLIST BOOKMARK—To celebrate the conclusion of your first year of reading together, create the bookmarks, listing the title, author, and date you read each book.

• HALL OF FAME—As you read more books, continue to compare and contrast characters from different books. Enjoy an ongoing nomination process for characters, such as the most inventive, the most thoughtful, the most creative, and other categories that encourage the girls to think of qualities that make people special or memorable.

- CRITICS' CHOICE—Ask for a volunteer daughter to write up the group's comments about a book that was considered particularly good, and check with the school or neighborhood library about posting the book review for others to enjoy. Create an annual list to share the same way.

- BOOK CLUB SCRAPBOOK—Create a scrapbook for the club, inviting girls to jot down their thoughts or draw illustrations about the books or the club to fill a page or two at each meeting.

- LET PICTURES TELL THE STORY—Contact local library, school, community hall, or nursing home to see about displaying art the girls might make illustrating a story or idea from a story.

- PLAY DETECTIVE—A hosting daughter might compile a list of riddles about characters or events in the story and begin discussion by asking the group to identify who or what she's describing.

- X MARKS THE SPOT—Enjoy a scavenger hunt without moving from your seat! Invite the girls to mark in the book or on a separate sheet of paper several words from the story that describe people, places, things, or feelings. If they jot the words on paper, be sure to tell them to mark where they found them. Then ask each girl in turn to name one of her words for the others to find.

we keep mother-daughter discussion first on our list, everything else we choose to do supports it, and every meeting becomes memorable.

ENDNOTES

📖 Good books are a treasure chest of ideas for activities.

📖 Book-related activities can bridge a gap between individual learning styles.

📖 Discussion—along with seeing, hearing, tasting, and touching stories—is an enrichment activity.

📖 Use the club to move beyond discussion of the books to the stories of your own lives: your history and dreams.

> "A lot of times books will lead to personal stories, don't be afraid to share openly."
>
> *Skylar*

THE END
WHERE NEW STORIES BEGIN

This story of our Mother-Daughter Book Club, like any story in a book, has to end a page before the back cover. But a very special and exciting part of the story only begins here. It's not a subplot or a sequel. It's the story that begins in another mother's heart, in another home, in another town, where the idea of a mother-daughter book discussion group takes root. Mother-daughter book clubs can flower anywhere and anytime the desire is there.

When one of Grace's friends moved to Swaziland, Grace suggested that she and her daughter start a mother-daughter book club there. They did, adopting our club's reading list as a starting point. Now we trade comments and opinions about books electronically by e-mail!

In Chicago, my writing partner Teresa Barker and her daughter, Rachel, nine, both insatiable readers, organized a mother-daughter book club with friends. After a move put forty-five minutes between them and their longtime friends, the club became a way of getting together at least once a month, along with a new friend Rachel introduced to the group from her new community.

Many of Rachel's ideas, and the experience of her club, have enriched this book and given our Mother-Daughter Book Club new ideas for book-related activities. Lynae Turner, one of the friends in Rachel's club, shares our group's African American heritage and has found a special delight in becoming a pen pal with Morgan and our club.

In reflecting on the needs of our girls, all of us have become more vocal advocates for them, and more eager to strengthen and celebrate the mother-daughter relationship. Progress comes in small steps and big ones. Any step you take toward shared reading and discussion with your daughter is a step in the right direction. Whatever you do, the rewards far outweigh the effort.

Maybe you'll organize a mother-daughter book club that meets monthly or quarterly. Maybe you'll bring up the idea within your neighborhood or religious community and encourage someone else to organize. Maybe you'll find just one other mother and daughter with whom to share reading and book chat over hot chocolate and cookies. Maybe for now, you'll simply find the time to read with your daughter, one book at a time, and at tuck-in time, ask: "What did you think of that story?"

Whatever you do, when you do, I'd love to hear about it. I see our group as an evolving circle of experience. If there's a better way to do something, or an interesting way to do something, we're eager to hear about it. Please visit our Web site www.themotherdaughterbookclub.com.

This circle of mothers and daughters can reach around the globe and into so many hearts and lives!

Where does it all end? It doesn't.

Let *your* Mother-Daughter Book Club story begin!

PART TWO

One of the best-kept secrets of Mother-Daughter Book Clubs is that young adult literature is so good, we mothers really enjoy reading the books as much as the girls do. In fact, so many wonderful books have been published since I wrote *100 Book for Girls to Grow On* in 1998, that choosing only fifteen books to include here was unbelievably daunting. My main criterion is that a book be a springboard to a fabulous discussion on a particular life issue. In some cases, the books had already passed this test: Four picks are books that Skylar's Mother-Daughter Book Club has read with great success.

First and foremost is *Whirligig* by Paul Fleischman. Since first reading it with the original Mother-Daughter Book Club, I have used *Whirligig* countless times when working with teens. It is my all-time favorite book for dealing with a myriad of adolescent issues, from teen drinking to girls accepting that it is okay to be smart. The discussions that have ensued are always insightful and varied and never cease to amaze me. I think it's telling that this was also the book Skylar chose to launch our new Mother-Daughter Book Club—it got us off to a great start!

Another no-brainer was Mark Haddon's *Curious Incident of the Dog in the Night-Time*—who doesn't like a good mystery? This one is a real category winner with a big twist. Christopher, the main character, is an autistic boy and the story is told through his eyes. The book does an outstanding job of letting you in to Christopher's world so you can appreciate it. Everyone in Skylar's book club loved this book.

Several of the books deal with more global themes that reflect today's world—a very changed world, as we all know, since 9/11. When I looked through *100 Books for Girls to Grow On*, I noticed plenty of books on war but absolutely none on terrorism. That's why I was thrilled to find Jonathan Safran Foer's

Extremely Loud and Incredibly Close. We seem to talk constantly about fighting terrorism, but what about the effect on our children's emotional well-being? Foer addresses the 9/11 tragedy through the eyes of a nine-year-old boy. His story made the tragedy seem much more real to those of us who were not directly affected.

Bel Canto by Ann Patchett also deals with terrorism but with multiple characters' perspectives and with viewpoints from both sides. I am eagerly awaiting the chance to discuss this book with Skylar's Mother-Daughter Book Club and to find out how much they, at fifteen and sixteen years of age, are willing to fight for what they believe in.

An ongoing problem in this country and around the world is racism. I believe it underlies a multitude of challenges we all face. By looking at skin color bias, Sharon Flake's *The Skin I'm In* provides a perfect entry point into a broader discussion of conflict. Although racism is often framed in terms of blacks and whites, *The Bean Trees* by Barbara Kingsolver deals with prejudice against Native Americans. Another much newer concern to reach global ears is female circumcision. *No Laughter Here* by Rita Williams-Garcia does an excellent job of presenting this very delicate subject. Where else but in the trusting, loving mother-daughter book club circle can young women discuss such horrific topics?

Coming-of-age stories abound and I selected several that I felt were particularly well done, with fully developed characters and enough plot twists and turns to keep the reader engaged: *Big Mouth & Ugly Girl* by Joyce Carol Oates; *Chu Ju's House* by Gloria Whelan; *Crystal* by Walter Dean Myers; *Hush* by Jacqueline Woodson; and *Speak* by Laurie Halse Anderson, which Morgan's club read when they were all in tenth grade.

Skylar's club chose Anderson's *Prom* instead of *Speak* and liked it equally well.

As in the case of Laurie Halse Anderson, often I discover a good book because I keep following a particular author's career and output. The original Mother-Daughter Book Club became particularly fond of Sharon Creech, for example. I read several of her more recent books for this new edition, and she did not disappoint. In the end I chose to include *Replay,* which is a great book for younger readers and stands out because it deals with the theme of how to get enough attention when you're part of a big family—and from a male perspective. It is always valuable yet rare for girls to view their lives through a new lens.

In addition to checking out other titles by an author you like, a good way to narrow your choices for a book club is by using the "If You Like This Book, Try . . ." feature. Each of the fifteen new discussion guides includes suggestions for further reading, just as I provided in the original edition and in *100 Books for Girls to Grow On*. I've indicated with an asterisk whenever these complementary titles are in *100 Books for Girls to Grow On*, where you will find detailed descriptions and discussion questions.

Another source for discovering excellent book club reads are bookstores. I highly recommend establishing a relationship with your local independent bookstore. You will find the staff extremely knowledgeable and always willing to help. My own private guide for more than a decade has been Jewell, who heads the children's department at my favorite bookstore, Politics and Prose. Several of the many books she suggested made my list. *A Northern Light* by Jennifer Donnelly and *True Believer* by Virginia Euwer Wolff are both great reads. When Skylar's Mother-Daughter Book Club discussed *A Northern*

Light, we talked about whether the mother's dying wish that her daughter take care of the family was fair. Most of us felt it was not fair, and the girls said they would never make any kind of dying wish.

I hope you enjoy sharing these selections with your daughters as much as I have enjoyed my hours with all the mothers and daughters in my book clubs.

Shireen Dodson,
2006

Replay
Sharon Creech

Twelve-year-old Leo gets a small part in his school play, but he dreams he's a great Broadway star. His big, boisterous family sometimes makes him feel like a sardine packed in a tin, but in his imagination, Leo is the center of attention and the pride of both his mother and father. Nicknamed "Fogboy" because he's always dreaming and replaying everyday scenes in his mind, Leo discovers a box in the attic that leads him to discover something real about growing up and something about his father and himself as well.

READING TIME: 2 hours; 240 pages

THEMES: dreams, imagination, family, family history

Discussion Questions

📖 Leo's brothers and sisters all vie for attention in their big Italian family, playing sports, singing, acting in school plays. Sometimes Leo feels anonymous among all the other family members. How different would it be if Leo was an only child? Can you relate to how he feels? In contrast, Leo's friend, Ruby, now an only child, says her life is like being under a microscope. With whom do you identify more, Leo or Ruby?

📖 Leo has lots of nicknames in the book. Fogboy. Sardine. Dreamer. What does Fogboy mean and how is it different from Dreamer?

📖 Leo's father is upset when he discovers Leo has found the box of childhood memorabilia in the attic. Why does Papa not want Leo to know what's inside? Would it have been better for Leo to ask his father directly for permission to read the journal?

📖 Mr. Beeber tells the cast to think about one of their siblings when the sibling was young and to compare that young version to the way the sibling is now. Try this same exercise with one of your own siblings or someone else you know well. Think about yourself when you were younger. How have you changed? Are there similarities between your young and your older selves?

📖 Leo has always thought that being a grown-up was the greatest thing in the world: "All that freedom to do whatever you want! You don't have a bunch of teachers telling you what to do, and you don't have to follow everyone else's rules, and you can stay up late and eat as many doughnuts as you want, and you can be whatever you want." What's wrong with this picture?

📖 Why was it so surprising for Leo to learn from his father's journal that his father used to tap-dance? Is there something in your life that you always do when you're happy? Or something in your life that always makes you happy when you do it?

📖 Why does Leo equate his father's not being happy now to being a father? Is Leo right or wrong about this?

📖 Leo says reading his father's journal is like reading a story about someone else. Why do you think this is so? How might the relationship with his children have been different if Papa had shared more of his childhood with them?

📖 Leo imagines himself to be many things—a great actor, writer, dancer, physicist, Nobel Prize–winner. How do these dreams help Leo in his everyday life?

📖 Leo remembers when he was little and his father used to tell him, Contento, and Pietro a story called "What We Did Today," making whatever they had done that day seem exciting and adventurous. How is this storytelling similar to Leo's own "replays"? What do you think the author is trying to say about storytelling?

📖 When Leo himself tells a "What We Did Today" story to Nunzio to stop him from crying, Papa says, "Leo, you make gold from pebbles." How else does Leo make gold from pebbles? How does his ability to do this affect the people around him?

📖 How does Leo's reading about his father's interests and goals in the journal help him to understand his father more? What is surprising to Leo about his father's childhood goals? Why does Leo scratch out all the goals on the list he makes for himself and change them all to "to be a father"?

📖 Leo imagines himself giving a press conference after having invented an automated house-cleaning robot and a cure for heart attacks. In his imagination, Leo accepts the Nobel Prize for these discoveries, saying he did it all "for his parents." If you could make discoveries to help specific members of your own family, what would those discoveries be?

📖 Leo is surprised to learn from Grandma that his father used to do plays when he was younger. What reason would the author have had for leaving this interest of Papa's off the list in the journal? What do you suppose Leo learns from this omission? When was Papa finally moved to tell Leo about his interest in plays as a child? Was this the right time for Papa to tell Leo?

📖 Why do you suppose Papa doesn't want to tell Leo how he got the scar on his neck?

📖 Why is it good for Leo and his grandmother to finally have a talk about Rosaria? What does Leo learn then about Papa and the family he grew up in? What does Grandma mean when she says of her conversation with Leo, "It upset me, yes, but it was a little good, too."

📖 How is Leo's friendship with Ruby important in this story? How are their lives similar? How are they different?

📖 Mr. Beeber asks the cast to do a banana rehearsal two days before the performance, with each cast member substituting the word banana in any one line of the play. How does this messing with the script help the players in their rehearsal? Would this work in real life?

📖 During the performance of *Rumpopo's Porch,* Leo worries that Rumpopo's sister might remind Papa, Grandma and Grandpa Navy of Rosaria and upset them. Name some other parallels between the characters in the novel and the characters in the story of Rumpopo?

📖 There are a number of symbols used throughout the novel. What do the tap shoes symbolize? What about the sardine? At the end of *Autobiography, Age Thirteen,* Leo sees a picture of his father standing on his front porch, smiling, with his arms spread. What does the porch symbolize? Does it mean the same thing in the play *Rumpopo's Porch?*

Beyond the Book

BANANA: Play a game in which book-club members substitute the word "banana" once each throughout the book discussion.

(It's important that each club member do the banana thing only once each so your meeting doesn't turn into a sillyfest!)

MEMORABILIA: In advance of your book-club meeting, ask members to create boxes filled with favorite childhood memorabilia. Bring the boxes to the discussion of *Replay*, and discuss how your younger selves are different from your older selves.

BROWNIES AND ICE CREAM: When Leo upsets Grandma at dinner, he imagines he is quarantined with no visitors allowed and that he doesn't speak ever again. When the doctor examines Leo's throat, he finds nothing that brownies and ice cream won't cure. Serve brownies and ice cream at your discussion of *Replay*.

If You Liked this Book, Try . . .

Walk Two Moons and *Chasing Redbird*, also by Sharon Creech

The Penderwicks: A Summer Tale of Four Sisters, Two Rabbits, and a Very Interesting Boy by Jeanne Birdsall

Criss Cross by Lynne Rae Perkins

About the Author

Sharon Creech is the author of the Newbery Medal winner *Walk Two Moons* and the Newbery Honor winner *The Wanderer*. After spending eighteen years teaching and writing in Europe, she and her husband have returned to the United States to live.

APPENDIX

BOOK LISTS FROM THE ORIGINAL MOTHER-DAUGHTER
BOOK CLUB

YEAR ONE 1995–1996   4TH GRADE

The Ear, the Eye, the Arm, *Nancy Farmer*
The Man in the Ceiling, *Jules Feiffer*
Charlie Pippin, *Candy Boyd*
The House of Dies Drear, *Virginia Hamilton*
Cousins, *Virginia Hamilton*
The Shimmershine Queen, *Camille Yarbrough*
Her Stories, *Virginia Hamilton*

YEAR TWO 1996–1997   5TH GRADE

The Mystery of Drear House, *Virginia Hamilton*
Julie of the Wolves, *Jean Craighead George*
The Friends, *Rosa Guy*
Homesick: My Own Story, *Jean Fritz*
Life in the Ghetto, *Anika Thomas*
Time Cat, *Lloyd Alexander*
Mama's Girl, *Veronica Chambers*
Rites of Passage, *Tonya Bolden*
Walk Two Moons, *Sharon Creech*

YEAR THREE 1997–1998   6TH GRADE

Absolutely Normal Chaos, *Sharon Creech*
The View from Saturday, *E. L Konigsburg*
Barrel of Laughs, Vail of Tears, *Jules Feiffer*
The Westing Game, *Ellen Raskin*
Something Terrible Happened, *Barbara Ann Porte*
Maizon at Blue Hill, *Jacqueline Woodson*
Another Way to Dance, *Martha Southgate*
A Warm Place, *Nancy Farmer*

YEAR FOUR 1998–1999   7TH GRADE

A Girl Named Disaster, *Nancy Farmer*
Sweet Whispers, Brother Rush, *Virginia Hamilton*
Confessions of a Wayward Preppie, *Stephen Roos*
African American Christmas Stories, *Betty Collier-Thomas*
The Red Scarf Girl, *Ji-Li Jiang*
Running Out of Time, *Margaret Peterson Haddix*
The True Confessions of Charlotte Doyle, *Avi*
Ella Enchanted, *Gail Carson Levine*
The Dark Side of Nowhere, *Neal Shusterman*
The Woman in the Wall, Patrice Kindl

YEAR FIVE 1999–2000   8TH GRADE

Holes, *Louis Sachar*
Bud, Not Buddy, *Christopher Paul Curtis*
Killing Mr. Griffin, *Lois Duncan*
Bluish, *Virginia Hamilton*
Habibi, *Naomi Shihab Nye*
The Moorchild, *Eloise McGraw*

Farewell to Manazanan, *Jeanne Wakatsuki Houston*
    & James Houston
The Skin I'm In, *Sharon Flake*
Death on the Nile, *Agatha Christie*

YEAR SIX 2000–2001   9TH GRADE

She Said Yes, *Misty Bernall*
A Ring of Endless Light, *Madeleine L'Engle*
Sugar in the Raw, *Rebecca Carroll*
Kindred, *Octavia Butler*
The Wedding, *Dorothy West*
Send Me Down a Miracle, *Han Nolan*
Rules of the Road, *Joan Bauer*
Lives of Our Own, *Lori Hewitt*
Whirligig, *Paul Fleischman*

YEAR SEVEN 2001–2002   10TH GRADE

Blanche Passes Go, *Barbara Neely*
If You Come Softly, *Jacqueline Woodson*
Calling the Swan, *Jean Thesman*
River Cross My Heart, *Breena Clarke*
A Stranger Is Watching, *Mary Higgins Clarke*
Speak, *Laurie Halse Amderson*

YEAR EIGHT 2002–2003   11TH GRADE

Searching for David's Heart, *Cherie Bennett*
White Oleander, *Janet Fitch*
The Just Us Girls, *Evelyn "Slim" Lambright*

Born Blue, *Han Nolan*
The Best American Mystery Stories of the Century, *Tony Hillerman*
The Sisterhood of the Traveling Pants, *Ann Brashares*
Kit's Wilderness, *David Almond*

BOOK LISTS FROM SKYLAR'S MOTHER-DAUGHTER BOOK CLUB

YEAR ONE 2004–2005   9TH GRADE

The Curious Incident of the Dog in the Night-Time, *Mark Haddon*
Prom, *Laurie Halse Anderson*
Extremely Loud and Incredibly Close, *Jonathan Safran Foer*

YEAR TWO 2005–2006   10TH GRADE

The Lovely Bones, *Alice Sebold*
Go Ask Alice, *Anonymous*
A Long Way Down, *Nick Hornby*
Bee Season, *Myla Goldberg*
Girl in Hyacinth Blue, *Susan Vreeland*
A Northern Light, *Jennifer Donnelly*
The Liar's Club, *Mary Carr*
The Ice Queen, *Alice Hoffman*

RESOURCES ON CHILDREN'S AND YOUNG ADULT BOOKS

ALAN Review
http://scholar.lib.vt.edu/ejournals/ALAN
The Assembly on Literature for Adolescents of the National

© 2006 by Harlee Little

About the Author

SHIREEN DODSON is a special assistant to the director of the Office of Civil Rights, U.S. Department of State. She is also active in her community, serving on the Board of Directors of the Anthony Bowen YMCA of Metropolitan Washington; Board of Trustees, Zion Baptist Church; and is Chair of the District of Columbia Retirement Board. She is an active member of the Washington Chapter of Jack and Jill of America, Inc., and was founding member of the Coalition of 100 Black Women of D.C., Inc. She lives in northwest Washington, D.C., and she is the mother of three children: Leroy III, twenty-five; Morgan, twenty; and Skylar, fifteen.

About the Writer

TERESA BARKER is a writer, editor, and communications consultant. She has written extensively about issues related to family, culture, education, and health. Her work has appeared in the *Chicago Tribune,* the *Chicago Sun-Times*, the *Eugene Register-Guard*, the *Nashville Tennessean,* and in other newspapers, magazines, and nationally syndicated publications. She is vice president and creative director of Readmore Communications in Chicago, which she founded with her husband, Steve Weiner. They live in Buffalo Grove, Illinois, with

ALSO BY
SHIREEN DODSON

100 BOOKS FOR GIRLS TO GROW ON

ISBN 0-06-095718-2 (paperback)

Shireen Dodson, author of the acclaimed *The Mother-Daughter Book Club*, offers a selection of both new and classic titles. Each book has been handpicked because it is a joy to read, because it inspires mother-daughter dialogue, and because it encourages creativity beyond the book experience. Included are brief plot summaries for each book, as well as thought-provoking discussion questions, inspired field trip ideas, fun crafts and activities, and biographies of the authors. You don't need to form a book club to use and enjoy *100 Books for Girls to Grow On*. Shireen Dodson offers stimulating ideas that will spark your daughter's creativity and nurture a love for books.